THE RIGHT FRAME

THE RIGHT FRAME

The Essential Guide to Framing

BY HENRY HEYDENRYK, JR.

The Lyons Press

Guilford, Connecticut

AN IMPRINT OF THE GLOBE PEQUOT PRESS

The Lyons Press is an imprint of The Globe Pequot Press.

Printed in Canada

10 9 8 7 6 5 4 3 2 1

Library of Congress Cataloging-in-Publication Data is available on file.

Book design by Casey Shain

PHOTOGRAPHY CREDITS

Photographs on pages 4, 15, 19, 21, 23, 25, 27, 29, 31, 33, 35, 37, 39, 41, 43, 45, 47, 51, 53, 55, 57, 59, 61, 65, 69, 71, 75, 79, and 81 courtesy of Art & Framing Council.

Photographs on pages 7, 9, and 77 copyright © Royalty-Free/Corbis.

Photographs on pages ii, 63, 73, and 83 copyright © 1999-2002 by Getty Images, Inc.

Photographs on pages 49 and 67 courtesy of Nathalie Guarracino.

Photograph on page 13, The Metropolitan Museum of Art, Bequest of Benjamin Altman, 1913, and Gift of Daniel Wildenstein, 1989. (14.40.642, 1989.132) Photograph © 1990 The Metropolitan Museum of Art.

Photograph on page 17, The Metropolitan Museum of Art, Robert Lehman Collection, 1975. (1975.1.124) Photograph © 1985 The Metropolitan Museum of Art.

Acknowledgments

The Lyons Press would like to thank the following for their generosity in supplying examples of the right way to frame:

Art & Framing Council
Kim Aherne, Executive Director
501 Maggiore Court
Brentwood, CA 94513
925.516.0313
www.artandframingcouncil.org

Nathalie Guarracino
New York, NY

Contents

THE RIGHT FRAME

Foreword

There are few aspects of interior design where there is a greater need for sound information and expert advice than in the presentation of art works. The framing, hanging, and lighting of paintings, drawings, and wall decorations of all kinds may establish the atmosphere of a room or a house, enhance or depreciate the quality of the pictures, and signify the owner's taste. It has been my experience that many people are casual, careless, or uninformed about picture framing. I feel that this book by Henry Heydenryk, a professional of experience and judgment, makes a contribution in an area where reference works are limited.

Whether or not you agree with G. K. Chesterton who said: "Art is limitation; the essence of every picture is the frame," there is no gainsaying the importance of this corollary to art. The picture framer's skill is a precise one, as invaluable as it is usually anonymous and unappreciated. The perfect frame is so suitable that it attracts no attention to itself.

The function of the frame is to protect the picture, to enhance it without entering into competition, and to make a transition between the limits of the picture and the wall it occupies or the composition with which it is involved. Aesthetically the frame should complement the subject matter it surrounds. Picture frames should be chosen with all these elements in mind, and Mr. Heydenryk ably discusses them in this monograph, which is dedicated to the whole concept of framing.

Fine picture frames are as well-designed and as durable as fine furniture. Quality or the lack of it is readily obvious in a picture frame, and to compromise is to defeat the purpose of art. It is wisdom to go to a specialist for the framing of good pictures and to take with you some understanding of the nature and scope of framing, as well as definitive knowledge of the wall and the room where your picture will hang. As well as complementing the subject matter of the painting, the frame should bear some relationship to other elements in the room, especially when it comes to scale, color, and style.

Picture frames are affected by changing fashions in interior architecture and home furnishings as well as by new styles, techniques, and approaches in painting. Modern painting has accounted for many changes in frame making—the use of new materials, new textures, and simplification of mouldings. Many modern artists have exhibited interest in the framing of their works to the degree of designing their own frames.

While a frame contemporary with the period of a painting is a safe assumption, the frame must be appropriate to the picture as well as historically correct. It is also possible to frame pictures satisfactorily in frames that derive from differing periods, if the effect is pleasing and other requirements of framing are fulfilled. In the popular "picture walls," instituted by interior designers to remedy the architectural monotony of long rectangular-shaped rooms in many modern apartment buildings, frames of various periods and styles can be juxtaposed effectively.

New framing of old pictures can give a new quality to interiors. Frames can become as dated as antimacassars, and Victorian hangovers in contemporary interiors are out of place. Updating the picture frames can change the quality of a room. Good pictures deserve the proper mounting, and an improper frame can obliterate a fine painting.

Interior designers will find Mr. Heydenryk's treatise especially useful, for the picture frame is an important adjunct in the creation of an effect often overlooked. One also hopes that professional framers will be spurred to new originality in their offerings by this volume, for we are often limited by what is available. The field offers unexplored possibilities for the designer.

For the collector or the owner of paintings, the study of this manual will give a new appreciation of his possessions. When choosing a frame, a primary goal should be the furthering of the artist's intention. If you accomplish this subjectively, the experience will give your picture new meaning for you.

WILLIAM PAHLMANN, F.A.I.D.

Introduction

A strange paradox exists today in the world of art.

On the one hand, it is evident that there has been a remarkable increase in the number of people interested in oil paintings, watercolors, fine photographs, and other types of pictures. On the other hand, it is astonishing that only a small proportion of these growing ranks of art lovers has any real concept of how to frame and hang pictures to achieve the best possible effect from what the artist has created.

A profile about me in *The New Yorker* magazine opened with these words: "Of all the long-suffering and self-effacing vice-regents of the arts whose primary function is to add lustre to somebody or something else—the accompanist to the soloist, the stage designer to the play, the second fiddle to the first fiddle—hardly any are less often honored by even incidental notice than the picture framer."

My colleagues and I are naturally concerned over this lack of recognition, but we take for granted that we have to undertake a certain amount of education to make the importance of proper framing better understood. We are concerned also with another aspect of the situation, mentioned or implied in several places in the article, that the selection of appropriate picture frames is either overlooked entirely, left to chance, or else so imbued with fetishism that the pictures themselves become secondary to the frames.

It would be unfair to ascribe the situation to the rapidly growing body of amateur painters and collectors, who could be excused for never having been informed about the role frames should play in art. In fact, the very need for this book arose from a minor crisis in the art world itself. A number of years ago, I was called upon by the Virginia Museum of Fine Art, in Richmond, to help solve a problem. The curators were so discouraged by the poorly framed entries of participants in the competitions for the Virginia Biennials that they asked me to prepare an exhibit. Their objective was to demonstrate the need for proper framing to prevent artists from partially destroying the very canvases they had created by using poor judgment and taste in framing.

Out of this situation grew an exhibit entitled, "Framing, Right and Wrong."

The exhibit traveled to hundreds of museums in almost every state in the Union. Its popularity is attested to by the fact that it was regularly booked ahead for a period of two years. It was well covered by the press; examples were displayed in magazines; and it appeared several times on television.

The purpose of this book is to explore, for beginners and established professionals alike, the "rights" and "wrongs" of picture framing, both in detail and in the broadest aspects of the subject. Since such intangibles as *taste, preference,* and *tradition* entered into the matter of framing—as in the case of any other area of the arts—there can be no absolute rights and wrongs. Some will perhaps take issue with my reasons for recommending certain types of frames for specific pictures and rejecting others. But I am firmly convinced that the contents of this book, the consideration of the many aspects of selecting appropriate frames, will go a long way toward providing any artwork with one important element of support that has been seriously lacking.

This is not a "How to" book. It will not show you how to make new picture frames, or even how to restore or decorate old ones. There are already several thoroughly detailed books in print on that subject. The objective of this book is, rather, to establish the concept of the picture frame in its rightful place, to stimulate interest in, and thoughtful consideration of, the selection of frames, and to serve as an aesthetic guide to better framing.

What Is a Frame?

The original "picture frame" was simply an opening in the forest foliage through which some prehistoric human looked forth on a scene appealing enough to capture and hold his attention for perhaps several minutes before he was distracted by something else. Such lookout points were revered by early tribespeople, leaf-framed bowers where traditionally only the chiefs or witch doctors were permitted to sit or crouch in isolated contemplation of the scene at hand.

At some unknown date in ancient history, it became the practice to frame a special setting by constructing a crude doorway of timbers, and later rocks, so that those entering would first have the impression of some natural entity contained within limitations set by man. The natural evolution was from rough slabs of stone, to the carved and massive doorways of the Egyptians, and ultimately to the arch, first perfected by the Assyrians around the seventh century B.C.

The important point here is that the picture frame, as a distinct element, originated with this whole concept of directing a viewer's eyes through a specially designed opening toward a scene entirely contained within the focal point of that opening.

In effect, the entrance to your home, an inviting doorway into a dining room, or a rose-clustered trellis at the near end of a garden are all frames. The same is true of a decorative fireplace, the proscenium of a theater, or the archway separating the nave from the sanctuary of a church.

This concept of viewing a scene through some kind of portal was actually carried over into artists' interpretations of early picture frames. In *Picture Framing*, a classic work on the art of frame making, Edward Landon points out that the earliest examples of frames were modeled after doorframes. He notes that "they were composed of two columns surmounted by a connecting entablature and this form persisted into the fifteenth century. Even the decorations painted by the artists around the edges of pictures before the introduction of movable frames were similar in form."

Going back to the earliest sculptured reliefs from Egypt, Persia, Phoenicia, and other ancient lands, we see examples of this kind of an attempt by artists to contain their work within a border. Many of these reliefs were framed by carved representations of temple doors or other formal openings actually in use at the time. Movable picture frames, as we know them today, date from the Italian Renaissance.

What is a frame? *Webster's New International Dictionary* describes it generally as "a kind of open case or structure made for admitting, enclosing, or supporting things, as that which encloses or contains a window, door, picture, etc.; that on which anything is held or stretched. . . . An enclosing border, esp. an ornamental one. . . ."

Frames can be as small as a coin, to encase a miniature portrait, or as large as the longest room, to set off a huge, extravagant mural. They can be as flat as a sheet of paper, or deep as an office desk. There is no limitation as to shape—oblong, square, round, oval, triangular, pentagonal, hexagonal, octagonal, or even so misshapen as to defy geometric classification.

For practical purposes, the components and elements of a standard picture frame can be broken down as follows:

MOULDING This is the basic element. Mouldings can be classified broadly into four categories: flat or angular, single-curved, multicurved, and compound. The latter may be a combination of curves and angles, or sometimes may be a combination of mouldings within mouldings.

DECORATION This may or may not be present on a moulding, in the form of carving, scratching, combing, metal or stone ornaments, or other artistic work that makes the overall design more complex. Many frames have plaster or composition ornaments or are decorated with veneer.

FILLET A fillet is a thin accent strip used on the inside edge of the mat or frame. Fillets are designed to complement the main moulding and add a distinctive touch to your finished piece.

FINISH There are two basic types of finishes: ones that are almost invisible, such as varnish, shellac, or wax, which are applied for purposes of *protecting* the frame; ones that are meant to be seen, such as white or colored casein paste paint, bronze powders, gold, silver or bronze metal leaf, or other coloring matter for *decorative* purposes.

MATBOARD These are flat pieces of cardboard, pressed wood, or other material, used within the outer moulding or frame to set off the picture and isolate it somewhat. Mats may be plain or decorated, colored or natural, uncovered, or covered with some textural material such as rough cloth or fine paper. Not all frames have mats, but when this element is used, it may be pencil-thin or extremely wide, depending upon the nature of the picture and the purpose of the mat.

BACKING Frequently confused with "mounting," backing is used, when necessary, as a support for the picture itself. Oil paintings seldom require backing, but delicate woodcuts or old engravings will need them. The usual cardboard or mat board will deteriorate and discolor with age, which then may also stain the paper of lithographs, drawings, and other graphic material. A backing, therefore, should be 100 percent rag content. Pictures should be attached to this board with inert paper "hinges," similar to those used in stamp albums. (*Note:* Many valuable pictures have been permanently stained by the improper use of various gummed tapes.)

GLAZING Available as glass or acrylic, this element is seen most often with watercolors, pastels, engravings, and other artwork that does not have any natural protection against dust and grime on the surface. Oil paintings seldom require glazing, except when in such ancient or poor condition that they could be ruined by the smallest accumulations of dust or dirt. Whenever and wherever used with pictures, glazing should be all but invisible, and so lighted that reflections do not spoil the effect of the picture itself. Glare-proof glasses and acrylics, though somewhat more expensive than the ordinary kinds, offer one method for solving the problem. The nonreflecting kinds have a slight opacity, however. This quality makes little difference on a black-and-white print or a strong watercolor, but it can blur a picture whose definition is not sharp to begin with, and to some degree, it flattens out delicate colorings.

RIGHT   *One of the earliest architectural uses of framing was the creation of elaborate surrounds for doorways. Entries to public buildings, the homes of the wealthy, and places of worship were decorated with columns, friezes, carvings, and painted designs, all indicating that something rare and special lay beyond the portal.*

LINER A linen liner is a fabric-covered frame that is sometimes used in place of a mat, generally used on oil paintings or needlework. Often called "inserts," these elements are the ones beneath and within the outer mouldings. They are used for a number of purposes: to give depth and dimension to the moulding; to form an extra, decorative border next to the picture; to serve as the separation between color and pattern of the painting and the frame; to reduce the size of a frame that is slightly too large for the picture itself.

BACKING PAPER Many pictures, particularly those that require glass on the front, are sealed in the back with a sheet of strong paper, tightly glued to the frame, and cut so that the edges are not visible. Backing paper simply protects the picture from dust and, to a limited degree, from changes in humidity. It is also sometimes useful for noting the date of the picture, place of purchase, cost, and other details you may want to record.

HANGERS The hanging unit on the back of a picture frame should be properly placed and adjusted, so that the picture retains an even position on the wall, and no lopsided stress is placed on the frame itself. Unusually large, or heavy, frames should be wired so that the wire is attached to two separate screw eyes, positioned about one-third of the way down from the top edge of the frame. (*Note:* Some thin frames can be given extra strength by stringing an additional wire tautly between two screw eyes on the vertical sides of the frame—or, if necessary, running from top to bottom.) So-called mirror hangers, which are attached by one or more screws and that lie flat against the back of a frame, are preferable for heavy pictures.

FITTING STRIPS Wooden or metal strips may be attached to the outer edge of a canvas or panel for protection. They should project approximately ⅛ inch above the painted surface so that the frame will rest on these strips and not press on the painting. This prevents damage to the surface due to pressure or friction and preserves the canvas from unnecessary wear.

Depending on the object that you are framing, you can sometimes break from traditional shapes. This shadow box featuring sports memorabilia is a playful pentagon.

A Brief Historical Sketch

In ancient times, the only real frames that existed were those used for hand mirrors or for setting off certain pieces of jewelry. One German authority stated that paintings were sometimes "framed" by being placed, freestanding, on decorated stands in wealthy homes long before the time of Christ. His findings, however, are based on illustrations within some surviving Pompeian wall paintings; no relics of such stands exist today.

Any realistic appraisal of the history of frames starts with the Middle Ages. Up until that time, oil painting had been considered not an independent art, but basically an *architectural* element. Then, in the thirteenth century, with the beginning of the Italian Renaissance, painters took to painting on panels—not only in Italy, but also throughout Europe. The earliest panel paintings had frames only in that the pictures were executed on the flat, slightly hollowed, surfaces of wooden sheets. The raised rim, often painted or decorated as a separate element, then served as the frame.

The next natural step in the development was for artists to paint a picture on a panel and then affix to it a surrounding rim of heavier wood. The real purpose was to reinforce the picture and to prevent the thin panel from warping, which would crack the painted surface.

In the late fifteenth century, Italian painters began to look upon their work as an independent art, no longer wedded to architecture, and significant enough for development in its own right. Many of the Italian master painters of the day became accomplished frame makers as well. It was only logical that framing itself should then develop as a serious art.

With the sixteenth century came an important milestone in framing. Patrons of the arts, who formerly had sponsored artists only for creating "great" works in cathedrals, churches, and occasionally public buildings, now began to hunger for art in their own homes. They commissioned portraits, allegorical representations, and other subjects of personal interest, which were then framed and hung in their own halls. In Italy, the rich merchants and nobles, such as the Medici in Florence and the Gonzaga in Mantua, poured such fortunes into the purchase of this kind of art that the demand for fine frames launched a thriving new business. Many painters, pressed with work, could do little more than sketch out the desired designs and pass along the frame-making assignments to their apprentices or to outside artisans.

THE LAST COMMUNION OF SAINT JEROME *by Botticelli (c. 1490) is a vivid example of how early artists typically surrounded their panel paintings with door-like architectural frames. These were often specifically designed for the artwork, and further helped to reinforce the wooden panel and keep it from warping.*

It has been generally accepted that the sixteenth century in Italy inspired some of the finest frames ever designed and made.

It is rather remarkable that the frames of this period exhibited such great taste and restraint, for the whole concept of framing at the beginning of the Italian Renaissance had stemmed from the way painting had been incorporated into architecture. The resulting frames, therefore, were almost literal reproductions of the niches into which the art had been placed. When removed from an ecclesiastical setting, frames that tried to reproduce architectural elements were so heavy and so elaborate against, say, an ordinary wall, that the paintings within were completely overshadowed.

The great masters of the sixteenth century somehow managed to avoid this exaggeration, designing frames that were completely harmonious with the paintings contained within them. But it was too good to last. In the late sixteenth century, frame-makers seemed determined to push their art for all it was worth. They carved elaborate mouldings, often cluttering them with "foreign objects," such as jewels, carved chunks of semi-precious stone, and bits of mirrored glass. All over Europe, fads began to spring up, as frame-makers tries to outdo each other by adding tortoiseshell, ivory, mother-of-pearl, and many another attention-getting substance.

The best of these elaborate frames—though too busy and restless for pictures—are not at all inappropriate for *mirrors*, where there is no constant image to cause interference. Venice, an important center for producing mirrors, was also the origin of many of the frames that we now classify as too overpowering and ornate for even the strongest oil paintings.

The moral here is that the frame's purpose is all-important to its design.

In the seventeenth century, Italian frame makers turned out more subdued designs, but leadership in the decorative arts passed over into France, where it was solidly entrenched until the time of the French Revolution. French frames of the period were imitated all over Europe, starting with the reign of Louis XI (1610–1643) and to a tremendous degree during the Golden Age of France in the reign of Louis XIV (1643–1715). Now, too, picture framing became firmly established as a separate craft. The noted Paris guilds were developed; standards were set and steadfastly controlled; and artisans concentrated on specialization. The frame-maker was a specialist within the already accepted profession of the cabinetmaker. Because of standardization, there is a certain sameness, however, in Louis XIV frames.

In the meantime, the Dutch were also perfecting the art of picture framing. While

In this shadow box treatment, the doorframe theme from the Botticelli painting is repeated in a modern context, giving this collectible doll an appealing showcase.

many of their designs were variations on the French, they did contribute some unique features. One was the use of exotic woods, such as ebony or mahogany, imported through the globe-encircling network of Dutch trade. Another was the development of a type known as the "border" frame perfected in the sixteenth century as the Lowlands interpretation of the Italian moulding.

Often, throughout history, the very technique of making a moulding has developed such artistry, or perhaps artisanship, that the frame has ended up half swallowing the painting. A talented Amsterdam goldsmith, Johan Lutma, for example, perfected a type of carved frame that in itself was a beauty to behold, with intricate little impressions of sea animals, birds, flowers, and other wildlife—all in high relief on a fairly flat moulding. The problem that resulted with the popularization of this type of frame—and more markedly with frames carved by less skillful artists than Lutma—was that many a fine painting found its strength weakened by an encircling array of trivia that distracted the eye.

The splendor and elegance of decoration reached a new height in France during the reign of Louis XV (1723–1774) as the decorative arts dominated the fine arts and frames became used everywhere. They appeared not only around pictures, but also on fire screens, in fabric designs, as elements of huge tapestries, for title pages of books, and even around commercial announcements. Swirls and undulations and leafy designs were found wherever a decoration was called for, and in many places where it was not.

Shortly after the middle of the eighteenth century, this kind of exuberant design gave way to the austere simplicity of neoclassicism, which spread quickly from its beginnings in Rome after the discovery of the buried cities of Herculaneum and Pompeii. In France, the new style was generally referred to as Louis XVI, continuing until the beginning of the French Revolution in 1789, after which France's influence over the arts went into a severe and prolonged decline.

Under Napoleon, at the beginning of the nineteenth century, frame making went into another stage of development. Much of the earlier classicism was retained during the Empire period, but there was a decided uniformity of design in most areas of art. The result was the precise, severe "scoop moulding" with plaster-cast ornamentation. The Empire frame is marked by perfect symmetry and exacting, harsh detail. While this kind of frame works well with many realistic paintings, Napoleon's overzealous championship of it left a long legacy in Paris. The curators of the Louvre spent many years replacing most of the Empire frames in which Napoleon insisted the exhibits there should be hung.

As this Nederlandish Virgin and Child shows, by the mid-sixteenth century, frames had become separate units from the paintings they surrounded.

Napoleon was not alone in his predisposition for uniformity. Many a more knowledgeable art authority than the Emperor fell into the pitfall of disregarding each painting as an individual work. Louis XII and Louis XIV frames were copied and turned out in assembly-line fashion as the nineteenth century progressed. Imitations of the carvings of the seventeenth century were so mechanically cast in plaster that they resembled iron. Bright gilding continued to be in vogue, so brash that it completely drew the eye away from the picture within.

Worst of all, it became the accepted practice among patrons of the arts to house large collections of paintings in *identical* frames, regardless of the subject matter, composition, or other elements concerned.

It was inevitable that eventually there should be a rebellion.

In the latter part of the nineteenth century, a group of artists began to defy the framing regimentation of the public and private galleries. They reexamined the function of the picture frame and found that the entire concept had long since become hideously deformed. Up until the 1870s, changes in taste and outlook had undergone a gradual metamorphosis, from good to bad to worse. Now the situation had become so intolerable that the artists concerned simply rejected everything that had gone before and started from scratch. It was like a return to the Middle Ages, when framing was an architectural element and a small group of artists realized that there was something wrong with the concept.

The result was the development of the Impressionist frame, often a simple moulding in white or white softened by small amounts of coloring. A few artists, notably Seurat and Degas, viewed the frame with such natural suspicion that they took to using simple, flat mouldings, on which they painted and speckled colors similar to the ones used on the canvases themselves, in effect, extending the painting outward a few inches.

America was spared a good many of the atrocities of overframing found in Europe for a good many years, mainly because there were few artisans and little machinery or tools for executing the elaborate frames of France and Italy. Many Early American frames were effective because of their stark simplicity, bordering pictures that in themselves bore the primitive stamp. But the floodgates were opened in America, as elsewhere, during the Victorian period.

"The frame-makers who constructed the monstrosities of the Victorian era," wrote artist Edward Landon, "were not content to put one heavily embellished gold frame around a picture of *The Stag at Bay* or something similar, but three or four. This birthday

While this is clearly a modern painting, the frame adheres to the method preferred by the Impressionists—simple white moulding softened with the addition of colors taken from the artwork itself.

19

cake was then enclosed in a glass-covered, plush-lined, mahogany shadow box. This was presumably for protection, but its need is a mystery since the interiors of that time were heavily shaded and hermetically sealed anyway."

After 1900, partly as a reaction against the extremes of Victorianism, picture frames tended to be less cluttered. The frames on geometrical paintings in particular, were reduced to little more than narrow bands. This trend might have continued almost until the present day had not the Paris Exposition of 1925 sparked a renewed interest in "Modern Art." After that date, the narrow mouldings gave way to frames that had more substance, and that bore some relationship to the pictures for which they were intended. In the 1930s, France, Belgium, and Holland produced not a few talented frame makers who created designs for the exciting new schools of painting that were blooming on all sides.

After the tragic interruption caused by World War II, a remarkably strong interest in the arts blossomed once more as many old art treasures were removed from their hiding places in war-ravaged lands. Frame making flourished once again—particularly in the United States.

Trends in frame making varied greatly during the second half of the twentieth century, from the minimalist "strip-framing" advocated by the Abstract Expressionists of the 1960s, to a return to the rich luster of gold and silver leaf in the 1990s. At the dawn of this new century, there are more choices and styles of frames available than ever before—and far fewer set-in-stone rules of right and wrong. Framers no longer focus on the Old Masters; the framers of today see a multiplicity of artwork enter their shops. From the standard terrain of limited-edition prints and original oils, they have ventured into the new territory of framing precious memorabilia: wedding invitations or babies' booties that commemorate a special occasion; wine labels or baseball cards that show off a collector's interest. Custom shadow-box framing has opened an even wider vista: sports memorabilia, antiques, Christmas ornaments—anything and everything can be set off to its best advantage in a well-chosen and well-made frame.

Although there are plenty of examples of bad, and tasteless, framing, it is encouraging to note the increase in good framing to be found in many homes and galleries. There is, too, tremendous excitement in current experimentation, in trying out new materials and textures and methods—not just for the sake of innovation, but also to provide new art styles with frames that enhance their values.

It is refreshing to feel, and to be convinced, that the art of framing is on the ascendancy.

*These days, frames are not just for prints and painting, but also for anything
precious that you want to display. This commodious shadow box is the
perfect setting for a beloved violin and box.*

The Nature of the Frame

The framing of a painting or drawing is a presentation of that painting or drawing to the best advantage. It is a means of defining and emphasizing the picture's area in relation to the larger area of the room. It should enhance, embellish, complement, and emphasize the picture. It should never overpower the subject. The frame acts as a sort of impresario; the picture remains the star performer, whether it's an original Botticelli or a Gauguin reprint.

Van Day Truex, a painter in his own right and former president of the Parsons School of Design in New York, made that statement in an article on how to frame and hang pictures. What Truex was concerned with in part—and what this chapter is devoted to—focuses on the *nature* of the frame. It is easy enough to define the physical makeup of a frame, and to isolate the various elements that go into it, but the interpretation is another matter entirely. Your overall impression of any specific frame will probably fit into one of the following three classifications:

◆   The frame will be sharp and distinct, setting off the picture with clearly defined lines.

◆   The frame will blend with the picture or the design, its definition soft or slightly out of focus, its style and design almost unnoticed.

◆   The frame will generally fit into the second category, but there will be certain sharply defined features—perhaps in the mat or the insert.

Selecting the right frame for a picture, while it is guided by certain factors of taste and style that will be discussed later, must be considered just as personal as choosing furniture for your living room or a major item of clothing. Too many people just "go out and buy a frame" whose inner dimensions are correct for the picture and whose price is within what they feel to be a reasonable budget. Surprisingly few do what any shopper does when buying shoes: try many of them on before choosing the right pair. Look at six, ten, a dozen different frames on the *picture* before making a decision.

22

Botanical prints are popular, inexpensive, and attractive additions to a wall or mantel. Here we see a tulip print framed simply in silver metal with a triple mat—black on the outer mat, with white and then black again—for a striking graphic treatment.

This time the framer has used a wide white mat combined with a narrow brick-colored mat, which picks up the hue of the flowers, and an inner mat of marbleized green, which plays off the color of the mitered-wood frame.

A reliable framer will not simply show you samples of mats and chevrons of moulding and expect you to make an on-the-spot choice. He will have on hand a wide selection of complete frames, to help you come to a decision. He will also help you to avoid the old myths that "all oils should be enclosed in gilded frames" or that "watercolors invariably require a wide mat to set them off against the background" or that "graphic prints are not properly framed unless bordered by a black moulding and a white mat."

There are, of course, thousands of different types and styles of frames—enough to confuse even an accomplished decorator. Nevertheless, the confusion is diminished if you bear in mind that there are only six basic categories to select from:

◆ Simple wood frames, whose attractiveness depends mainly on the kind of wood grain, its color, finish, and texture.

◆ Frames whose mouldings are contoured with composition, gesso (plaster, or similar), and whose finish is either plain or patterned.

◆ Frames finished with gesso, but with additional carving, gilding, or other ornamentation.

◆ Hand-carved reproductions of frames from specific periods, such as Italian Renaissance or Louis XIV.

◆ Actual antique frames.

◆ Metal frames, plastic-coated frames, or combinations of plastic, metal, and wood.

After selecting a style or period, the next key consideration is one of *proportion*. The width of the frame, on the one hand, has to be substantial enough to suit the size, subject matter, and medium of the picture. On the other hand, you don't want it so wide that it squashes the picture or overpowers it. Because of subject matter and palette, many paintings look *larger* or *smaller* than they actually are. They must be framed accordingly.

While it is true that certain periods in the history of art have generated certain types and styles of frames, one popular misconception should be corrected: *The period of the painting or reproduction does not necessarily determine the style of the frame.*

The situation parallels that of the woman going out to buy a new dress (if we may use that old metaphor again). If she is overweight, she selects colors and styles that minimize the poundage. If she is too thin, she selects a "frame" that will give the reverse

Our tulip print gets a more ornate treatment—
a wood and gesso gilt frame. The wide mat is a
textured taupe; the narrow mat is rust-colored
with a fillet of gold that matches the inset on
the frame.

For the ultimate in elegance, the print has now
been set in an elaborate gilt frame, and matted
in deep, rich olive with a striking surround of
mitered gilt.

effect. Your selection of a frame, and the matting that goes with it, must be influenced by what artists sometimes refer to as the "weight" of the picture itself. This term has nothing to do with the avoirdupois of the picture. Rather, it is concerned with the colors, the strength of the hues, and the composition. An oil painting with heavy, dark areas of color would obviously require a different frame from the same subject—even the same square footage of surface—rendered with delicate strokes, or in pastels.

The width of the frame has been mentioned above. Less obvious to the viewer, but of equal importance is the depth of the frame, that is, the dimension from the outermost part of the moulding to the part that touches the wall.

The nature of the frame is also considerably determined by one fairly down-to-earth factor: the type of material used for the moulding. Besides plain or carved wood, the most familiar (though not necessarily the most understood) material is gesso. Gesso, which means "chalk" or "plaster" in Italian, is basically finely ground chalk mixed with a glue solution that can be readily worked by knowledgeable craftspeople and that dries into a hard, durable finish. Its only real disadvantage is that it tends to be brittle, and hence can be chipped during transportation or storage.

Gesso has been popular down through the centuries in the art world because it is easy to obtain, inexpensive, and an extremely flexible medium for artistic creativity. For example, here are a few of the methods of transforming globs of soft gesso into works of art. Gesso can be . . .

◆ mixed with coloring matter to achieve either a uniform or an uneven stain throughout.

◆ surface-colored with gold-leaf gilding or a patina.

◆ imprinted with almost any two-dimensional design—from coins to carved symbols to the texture of coarse-grained cloth against the surface.

◆ shellacked, glazed, and waxed.

◆ combed (with an ordinary comb or notched metal) and scratched (with any sharp instrument).

◆ ingrained with foreign objects—metal flakes, glass, sand, and so on.

◆ carved with an artisan's tool

◆ stippled with a wet brush, branch, or other common device.

A prime example of gilt gesso moulding highlights this Renoir reproduction of
TWO SISTERS ON THE TERRACE. *For centuries, gesso has been a favorite*
of frame makers for its accessibility and flexibility as a medium.

◆ mixed with reinforcing materials (such as fiber or rosin) to make a malleable material that can be cast or pressed from molds.

A brief description of the gesso process has been included here, not to try to stimulate do-it-yourself efforts (gesso is highly popular with artists who like to make their own frames, because of its flexibility), but to provide a better understanding of the *nature* of the frame and one of the most familiar materials in its makeup. Understanding the materials helps greatly in determining the best frame for a picture—just as understanding various fabrics helps a decorator select furniture.

A good picture frame should be as durable as fine furniture. It has to be if it is to fulfill its primary practical function: to protect the picture. Despite this durability, there are few old paintings that still retain their original frames. This situation is not so much a result of deterioration or damage as it is a consequence of changing tastes. Old Masters were frequently taken out of their original frames to be reframed in a style more in vogue with a later era. As a result, the artistry of picture framing has been much maligned down through the ages, with fads and crazes taking over the function that should have been exercised by good taste.

Many years ago, art critic Peyton Boswell wrote in a magazine article:

> Of all the transgressions of good taste and common sense that have been made in the sacred name of art, those connected with the framing of pictures are perhaps the most flagrant. [The United States] especially has been a hard offender. Just as our forbears used to obscure the female form in horrible hoopskirts, so they were wont to ensconce their pictures in heavy, ornate frames and—save the mark!—they even hid away both frame and picture in a tunnel called a "shadow box." This last-named monstrosity has almost disappeared, to come forth only now and then when paintings are brought out of old houses to be put up at auction sales. But the ornate and vulgar frame is with us still, casting its blight on whatever painting it can find to obscure and rob of its true effectiveness.

The situation has not changed much since Boswell's agonized outcry in the early 1920s. While the public displays a greater and greater interest in artwork of all kinds—along with the same traditional neglect of good framing—examples of bad framing continue to plague us.

What can be done about it?

A great deal!

As can be seen in this simple and charming display of ballet shoes, the modern shadow box no longer resembles the Victorian nightmare of grotesquely elaborate collections under glass.

The Frame and Its Relationship to the Picture

There are four aesthetic reasons for framing a picture: to focus and limit the eye on the composition of the picture itself; to reinforce significant, but sometimes elusive, elements and color tones in the picture; to increase the size of the picture; and to serve as a transition between the picture and the wall behind it.

The most important consideration is the relationship of the frame to the picture.

It is an odd, but interesting, paradox that artists themselves are often frustrated when selecting the proper frames for their works of art. One of the first to make a determined effort to overcome this helplessness was James McNeill Whistler, who was continually finding his delicately toned paintings hung in heavy, discordant frames. He was finally driven to making, designing, and painting his own frames. To make sure that the owners of his paintings did not destroy the effect he wanted to achieve, by discarding the original frames and buying new ones, he started the practice of signing many of the frames with the familiar Whistler "butterfly." This added so much to the value of the entity, that few owners would even consider making a change of frame from that time on.

Another successful artist-frame maker was the Boston landscapist Herman Dudley Murphy. "So successful was he in framing his own pictures," reported one critic, "that he was asked by brother artists to apply his ideas to other pictures."

Murphy, who was referred to as "the Dean of American Picture Framers," bucked one of the framing trends of the 1920s (one that unfortunately persists to this day). He noted that "to frame pictures of different styles alike in one design of frame is to kill their individuality." The right frame enhances what lies between its borders; the wrong frame obscures it. "You may spoil absolutely the effect of a fine picture by an unsuitable frame just as you may make an almost poor one look distinguished by a proper setting," he continued. "Put a delicate, subtle Whistler nocturne in a glittering, heavily ornamented frame and hang it on a wall with a lot of other pictures and you will never see it. Put a simple flat frame of parallel lines upon a sumptuous Venetian subject of the style of Titian or Veronese and it would at once cheapen the picture and make it look almost tawdry."

When displaying collections, there are two equally successful methods—you can choose to showcase one special item, as seen here in the top photo with its single postage stamp artfully matted, or you can select a number of items and arrange them in an attractive random pattern as seen in the lower photo.

It is easy to look at frames critically, or to quote established authorities (as above) on what *not* to do, but it's not so simple to discuss the subject constructively and suggest how to go about correct framing. Going back historically for a moment and approaching the subject from a "don't" point of view, one misconception about framing that has come down through the ages is that frames are *architectural* elements. While it is true, as will be discussed in the next chapter, that frames have to harmonize to some degree with the setting, they cannot primarily be considered from that viewpoint—that is, before the relationship of frame to picture has been carefully considered.

There was a time when a decorator, having once decided that the interior of a home should be "French Provincial" or "Early American" or some other style, was then convinced that the furnishings—including all picture frames—should be in the same style. Just imagine a formal, heavily gilded Louis XIV frame on a simple Grandma Moses primitive and you can see the effect of that rule! Today, it is widely accepted that any home—even individual rooms—can be a mixture of styles and periods, when there is a harmonious blending of elements and colors. Even so, many owners of fine paintings, perhaps knowledgeable when it comes to the selection of art, will have such a vague concept of the art of framing that they will have only one criterion to guide them: the style of the furniture in a room. They therefore will let their judgment be guided far more by the traditional old architectural viewpoint than by the particular requirements of individual pictures or objects.

Without knowing the first thing about the complexities of styles and periods in art history, you can come close to the selection of the proper frame just by studying the demands of the picture itself. Ask yourself whether or not there should be a marked transition between the picture and the moulding. An oil that has great depth will often have that depth distorted if the moulding is too close to the edges of the composition. The frame may absorb the dimensionality of the painting. Therefore, by experimenting with different frames, you will begin to see that the ones with an insert or certain type of mat are more successful at retaining—and better yet, emphasizing—the depth of the painting.

For a picture that has this three-dimensional effect, it will usually prove most effective to have a moulding that slants *inward* (toward the composition), regardless of the type of mat or insert, to enhance the dimension. Conversely, if the composition is flat, two-dimensional, as in the case of most paintings classified as "abstract art," mouldings

A static object can become a work of art when framed dramatically. Here black-distressed silver moulding mimics the mesh of a vintage purse and its inner beading echoes the chain strap. A velvety black mat contrasts with the luster of the purse.

33

that are flat or slant *outward* (receding toward the wall) will be appropriate. They avoid the common mistake of using a frame to introduce depth to a picture that has little or no such dimension.

The matter of coloring is another point that can be of far greater importance than trying to match periods. Harsh coloring or shiny gilding on a frame, appropriate for some pictures, can easily drain much of the essence from a picture that otherwise would be lively and brilliant. A delicate overtone on the frame will serve to bring out subtle colorings within the composition. Here again, an insert or liner can help to separate related tones in picture and frame. Study so-called "black-and-white" prints or antique engravings, or closely examine paintings that are classed as "monochromatic." Instead of just one color, you will find the essence of several hues, all of which can be brought out and enhanced by the proper frame.

"Gold and black are always safe colors for pictures that have no real color," an artist said to me one day. Perhaps, but how much better to effect the skillful use of shades of brown and gray, or touches of metallic leaf that will strengthen the picture instead of merely border it!

Writing in *Plaisir de France*, artist Jean-Pierre Guerin made the point that a good frame not only harmonizes with the picture but also helps to develop and prolong the vision of the artist. Each element within the frame—size, design, color, makeup—should be thought of as something you can employ to "prolong the vision."

Take the matter of coloring. If a careful and considered study of a picture reveals delicate colors that might easily be overlooked by a more casual viewer, the frame-maker should consider what those colors, or their complements, could do for the picture when blended into the frame.

Again, without getting into the concern over period and style, you can determine the proper size and weight for a frame by a simple, realistic consideration of the subject matter itself. Each picture, each composition has a definite "weight quality." Just as a matter of example, architectural subjects certainly tend to be far weightier than, say, even the boldest still life. Portraits of children are normally much more lightweight than portraits of their parents. A peasant scene is likely to be at home in a sturdy, substantial frame; whereas a composition showing ladies at a dance would be overpowered by this kind of frame.

Even the arrested motion of a feeding hummingbird conveys movement. When displaying
pictures with a strong sense of motion, it is best to keep the frame treatment simple—
forceful enough to contain the art, but without any distracting fussy elements.
Here the image has space to fly in a wide swath of white matting surrounded by a
thin fillet, which repeats the ornate gilded moulding.

35

Another factor that may influence a decision about framing is the matter of movement. This is a difficult term to define, because there are so many different types of movement. The subject itself can be in motion, as in the case of Toulouse-Lautrec's poster of can-can dancers, *La Troupe de Mlle Églantine*. The colors can be lively, as in most of Gauguin's works. The lines can be in complex movement, as in Marcel Duchamps' painting, *Nude Descending a Stairway*.

At any rate, no matter what the type of movement, it is fairly safe to say that the more there is of it, the stronger the frame containing it will have to be. When you see a picture with a great many horizontal lines and conventional elements it is likely to require less strength in the frame than a picture that has diagonal lines, violent movement, or other restless features.

The mood of the composition has to be considered as well. Romantic, gentle subjects such as Monet's *Water Lilies* call for more delicate frames than do those that are realistic and matter of fact. Surrealistic, fanciful subjects, such as those painted by Salvador Dali, allow more inventiveness and daring than other types in the use of framing materials.

It has been mentioned that frames are useful in helping to increase the size of a picture. This is a feature, however, that has been rashly misused. You can find, without too much trouble, many pictures in homes, offices, and even galleries that have been ridiculously overframed, simply because the wall space seemed to call for a larger artistic element than could be produced by the picture in a properly proportioned frame.

Another grievous practice is that of trimming down a picture to fit a frame already on hand or found in grandma's attic. Remember that a picture of any real value has a size, shape, and proportion exactly determined by the artist himself. These qualities are as important to the picture, whether you like them or not, as the artist's choice of colors and the technique used in the rendering. To cut a picture to fit a frame is even more of an aesthetic crime than to select the colors for a matting strip because they happen to match the fabric of your new sofa!

Some of the "rights" and "wrongs" will be more easily understandable through a study of the visual examples in this book. The noted Degas once remarked to painter Moise Kisling, "The frame is the reward of the artist." To add a missing element to his statement, it should be pointed out that "a good frame is also the enduring reward of the owner of the picture."

When trying to create a calming aura with your framed artwork, simplicity is key. Here, an unadorned gilt frame and velvety black mat echo the serene mood of this landscape photograph.

Ten Commandments for the Proper Framing of Pictures

1   *The width and pattern* of the moulding must bear relationship to the design and "weight" of the picture. A painting with simple, uncomplicated design calls for a plain moulding; a much-detailed composition is best balanced by a rich design in the frame, with ornamentation called for.

2   *A receding moulding* (one slanting toward the wall) or a rather flat profile will suit two-dimensional paintings best.

3   *A concave moulding* (one slanting toward the painting) will enhance the feeling of perspective suggested by a composition in depth.

4   *Strong, bold patterns* (such as in Van Gogh's paintings) demand powerful lines in the frame, to contain the composition.

5   *A delicate, feathery, airy composition* (such as a Degas) calls for the same "frivolous" feeling in the frame.

6   *A linear composition* (such as a Mondrian) calls for a repeat of this fine, lineal quality in the frame.

7   *Inserts, or contrasting colors,* will help to separate the ornamentation or pronounced color in a frame from those in the picture and will enhance the feeling of perspective.

8   *Mats for watercolors and prints* should be chosen to accentuate the significant colors. White is seldom right, because it tends to flatten the picture and darken it by contrast.

9   *Only in the matter of glass protection* do pastels and watercolors call for special treatment. A gouache can be as strong in color and pattern as any oil, and should be framed accordingly.

10 *Key the colorings in frames* to hues in the picture. A general guide is that warmly toned pictures (in which reds, browns and yellows predominate) are most appropriate in warm-toned frames; whereas cool colors (blues, greens, blue-blacks, whites) are likely to go best in frames that have silvery or similar cool tones.

Imaginative matting can make all the difference between blah wall art and a really vibrant

presentation. In this print of poppies, the basic black frame gives way to a wide field

of blue mat, beveled to reveal a black core, then combines a narrow mat of

orange with another of blue. The framer clearly used color for the maximum effect,

letting the bright mat layers reflect colors found in the artwork

The Frame and Its Relationship to the Background

There is an interesting and lively passage in Irving Stone's book *Lust for Life* that recreates a discussion between Georges Seurat and several other noted contemporary artists of his day. Seurat is speaking.

> "... We get through with a canvas. Then what do we do? We turn it over to some fool who puts it into a hideous gold frame and kills our every last effect. No, I propose that we should never let a picture out of our hands until we've put it into a frame and painted the frame so that it becomes an integral part of the picture."
>
> "But, Seurat, you're stopping too soon. Every picture must be hung in a room. And if the room is the wrong color, it will kill the picture and frame both."
>
> "That's right. Why not paint the room to match the frame?"
>
> "A good idea," said Seurat.
>
> "What about the house the room is in?"
>
> "And the city that the house is in?"
>
> "Oh, Georges, Georges, you do get the damndest ideas."
>
> "That's what comes from painting with your brain."

This little interplay of artistic exaggeration is quoted here as a way of pointing out that a picture frame has a responsibility far more complex than simply holding an object of art on the wall. In addition to serving its primary function of bringing out the best qualities in a picture, the frame has the secondary task of forming a graceful transition from surface to surface, regardless of what the situation, position, or materials happen to be. Sometimes there must be a compromise in order to achieve the best and most fitting overall presentation of the picture concerned. It would be unrealistic to assume that a picture

40

The simple version of our framed botanical print is right at home with modern furnishings,
especially in rooms that make use of black-and-white as their décor theme.

can be wedded to the best possible frame in the frame maker's studio and invariably be transported to its ultimate home with an absolute guarantee that it will be "right."

The question may, and frequently does, resolve itself into a debate as to which is more important, the painting or the decor of the room.

Looking at the relationships and values, we can find a number of instances in history, as well as in contemporary thinking, where pictures—even Old Masters—have been considered as a mere element of decor. For example, William Morris, the English writer, poet, artist, socialist, decorator, and general critic of his day, was highly successful in pioneering a movement that looked upon painting as no more of an art than any other phase of architecture or interior decoration. It was perfectly valid, he contended, to design frames as part of the entire interior style, and then put paintings or other pictures in them, according to personal taste and desire.

Such thinking ignores the commonly accepted belief today that aesthetically pleasing interior decor does not necessarily have to fit a pattern, be determined by a formula, or adhere strictly to one historical period throughout. "If a seventeenth-century frame turns out to be best for a picture, it should be framed that way, even in a modern room," says Bertha Shaeffer, owner of an art gallery and herself recognized as a leading decorator. As for groups of pictures, she adds that they can be hung together in *different* frames entirely, as long is there is some harmony of relationship.

People tend to become nervously confused when confronted with the problem of whether they should have frames that are "modern," "contemporary," "traditional," or "antique." Yet, all styles are related. A study of the makeup of a number of modern mouldings will show that they are basically adaptations of conventional mouldings of a past age. The quotation from Ecclesiastes, "There is no new thing under the sun," is as applicable to frames as it is to just about any other object on earth.

The appropriateness and modernity come, not through innovation, but through the fresh approach and natural application of elements and designs. That is one reason why it has been proven that furniture, furnishings, and art of different periods can be mixed when imaginatively integrated.

In the relationship of picture to surroundings, framing plays a decisive part in determining the *importance* of the picture. A heavy frame can make an oil painting more dominant than it otherwise would be. If it were appropriate to frame a print in a wood moulding, and if that same moulding were then used elsewhere in the room as

42

The wood framed print blends well with natural wood furniture, such as the oak sideboard shown here. This relaxed country look works perfectly in the kitchen or family room.

an architectural feature, the picture would be less dominant than if its frame were unique to the surroundings.

The background helps to determine the strength and importance of the picture. A busy background, such as a flowery wallpaper, would not be appropriate for most pictures, with the possible exception of large, strongly colored oils. Even so, the hues in the background, unless carefully selected to complement the art, would prove distracting and create an undesirable restlessness. Surely here the frame should isolate and separate picture from background more noticeably and distinctly.

Texture makes a difference, too. Whereas a rough, burlap wall covering or Japanese grass cloth might be suitable behind large, strong-compositioned pictures, they might drain the beauty from more delicate ones. The sheer starkness of smooth white plaster can help to add aesthetic impact to a dramatic scene; but it can also be overly dramatic if the subject of the picture happens to be fragile in nature.

A small frame can be made to look larger and a large frame smaller by the type and coloring of the wall. Contrasting colors will make the picture stand out, whereas harmonious colors will tend to absorb it, and reduce the apparent size of the frame.

With so many elements playing a part in determining the picture's importance, it is not hard to see that you have considerable flexibility in deciding what degree of strength the picture should have. It can be practically thrust out at the viewer, dramatized by the color and texture of the wall, and by the amount of space around it; or that same picture and frame can be absorbed, subdued—even destroyed—by the treatment of the surroundings.

An interesting and exemplary case history of picture vs. surroundings comes up in considering what to do about abstract paintings, which are two-dimensional and fairly simple and clean in composition. A few years ago, the problem of framing and hanging them was not so widespread because interiors tended also to be simple and uncluttered. Today, however, there is a definite trend toward the "rich" interior—rich in texture, in furnishings, and in the number of objects scattered about. The argument has been set forth that many abstract paintings are so huge that they are either, a) physically very difficult to frame, or, b) far too costly to frame. In either case, there is no sound artistic reason for omitting frames unless the surroundings can suitably serve the same purpose.

These abstracts can often be appropriately framed in wide mouldings of beautifully textured old chestnut, rather flat, with hand-carved designs inspired by stylized pat-

44

The elegant treatment of this botanical print, with its gilt frame and textured mat, makes it ideal for use in a study, office, or formal dining room.

terns of African, Polynesian, and Indonesian origin, combined with a definite, sharp out-line around the canvas proper. These frames are entirely appropriate to the luxury of the surroundings, on the one hand setting off the art dramatically and, on the other hand, isolating the paintings from the distracting features of other art in the room, large lamps, or exotic plants.

Reproductions of art should be treated with as much respect as originals when it comes to selecting frames. Naturally, most reproductions vary slightly from the originals in subtle toning, in "weight," and occasionally in size. The approach to framing, however, should be exactly the same.

Truly modern mouldings for modern paintings are available, making it easily possible to find a suitable frame. We are not forced to limit our selections to strips of wood, metal, or plastic, but can find forms that will function harmoniously and unobtrusively. Often a modest moulding with an insert or liner will best fulfill the requirements of painting and surroundings—or a rather narrow band surrounded by flat, textured wood to provide the desired separation.

The print, framed with opulently carved gilt, is now the perfect accessory for your foyer

or living room. It looks equally impressive mounted over a console table or

displayed above an ornate fireplace.

Proper Lighting

In the appendix to the scholarly work *The Care of Pictures* by George L. Stout, there is a section that reads as follows:

> COLOR MEASUREMENT. All measurement of visual tone in pictures is based on means to record the quality and quantity of light which can be reflected from a specific, uniform tonal area. The quantity is the total amount of light, regardless of color. Specific color is the quality of light reflected. A rough or approximate estimate of color measure for a given tone can be made by means of comparison with known samples.

The text refers basically to the use of color measurement in determining the condition of Old Masters, and is for the most part highly technical. The quotation is made here to lead into a discussion of the importance of proper lighting, not only so that viewers can better see framed pictures, but so that they can see the true colors, as applied by the artist, and with the values he intended.

Picture frames bear a direct relationship to lighting.

For one thing, their shape, depth, coloring, and reflective qualities can attract light to, or deflect it from, the surface of the picture. For another, their physical makeup determines how far out the subject hangs from the wall, and whether it is precisely perpendicular or slightly inclined. An important factor in the relationship is the nature and amount of color in the moulding. This can effect subtle (and some-times unwanted) changes in the tones of the picture.

Have you ever noticed how a soft, white sweater can take on a visible glow of color when the wearer has a brightly colored purse, or other reflective object in hand? Paintings can be equally influenced, and with good or bad effect, depending upon the skill (or lack of it) that has gone into the selection of the frame.

It is traditionally considered that the best light for paintings is natural *light*, or at least some form of illumination that closely approximates that of nature. The reasoning stems from the assumption that most artists paint under a skylight, during the daytime, and preferably with the glass facing north. Hence, the colors and tones and shadings

This oil pastel by New York artist Nathalie Guarracino benefits from its mitered gilt frame, which draws the eye to the golden swashes and dapples in the artwork, creating a dynamic energy between image and frame.

which they create under these conditions can be considerably distorted by artificial light, almost as much as though you were to view the work through a pair of tinted glasses.

It is therefore somewhat ironic that art in the home is hung in rooms that are occupied probably three-quarters of the time in the evening and where artificial light must be the prime consideration in the placement and treatment of the subjects. It is, in fact, rather astonishing that art can be properly appreciated at all in the home when you consider the multiple factors involved, such as differences in lighting fixtures, wide variations in the size, shape, and coloring of rooms, the hundreds of types and wattages of bulbs available, and individual ideas as to just how an object on the wall should be illuminated to begin with.

The Old Masters had no such problem. Artists knew exactly where their works were to be hung. In many instances, they painted them right on the scene, frequently on the wall itself. Today's painters usually have little idea where their works may end up—in a well-skylighted gallery, a darkly paneled drawing room of an old brownstone house, the modern living room of a ranch house in the suburbs. Therefore, it is entirely up to the purchaser to interpret the artist's intent and to determine the lighting conditions under which the picture will be shown.

Fortunately, today's technology has created artificial lighting whose values are close to those of daylight. Many galleries and exhibits successfully use forms of fluorescent lighting shielded by milky plastic to simulate the daylight, which, architecturally, it may be impossible for the hall to have. While this effect is seldom achievable in the home, there are at least five methods of lighting that are practical for home use:

- Overhead fluorescent, or other lighting fixtures set into the ceiling to simulate a skylight.

- Ceiling spotlights, with pinhole openings, that are unobtrusive, yet focus regulated light on the picture.

- Wall spotlights, which are more noticeable, but that achieve the same effect as ceiling spots.

- Long "pencil" or "finger" lights set in brackets over the picture, and usually attached to the frame.

- Lights similar to No. 4 above, but with the brackets attached to the *bottom* of the frame.

Although most original paintings are created in natural light, unfortunately most artwork in the home is displayed under less-forgiving incandescent light.

There has long been controversial discussion in the professional world of art about the best type of artificial lighting for home use. "*Over* the picture is generally better," says one school. "*Under* the picture is less obtrusive and gives the same effect," says another. "Lights never should be *on* the picture, but at a distance from it," insists a third group.

The only realistic approach is to experiment with a given picture, in its frame, until the right lighting effect is achieved. A spot strengthens some compositions; other compositions require an absolutely even diffusion of light throughout.

A minor point, but one that can often cause great detraction, is the subject of wiring, when the light is attached directly to the picture. Nothing looks more incongruous than an object of art on a wall, trailing a drooping, sloppy light cord. At the very least, the cord should run straight down from the center of the picture, and be painted to blend as much as possible with the wall.

In the case of valuable paintings, proper lighting is not only important for the sake of illumination, but for the protection of the picture. As Stout says in his work on *The Care of Pictures*:

> Excess light, especially direct sunlight or prolonged daylight, will fade certain colors and will hasten the darkening and weakening of the cellulose fiber in paper and fabric. Unbroken darkness causes discoloration of oils and augments the development of mold and fungi.

It is possible to set a small light inside a shadow box to dramatize an object.

Here, a simple black mailbox gains dimension and flair.

The Right Frame for Any Artwork

Thus far, the text has discussed framing broadly in relation to the "picture," with occasional reference to more specific media, or what Webster defines as "a representation, as of a person, group of objects, landscape, building, or the like, on canvas, paper, or other surface, produced by paintings, drawing, engraving, photography, etc. . . ."

Naturally, the medium used by the artist is one of the factors in determining the nature of the frame. This chapter is a cataloging of the most important and familiar media, with brief notes on guidelines for framing each kind. Comparisons are helpful in judging rights and wrongs. Nevertheless, "The Ten Commandments for the Proper Framing of Pictures" listed in Chapter 4 should always be taken into account. The following paragraphs are merely general comments.

OILS OR ACRYLICS These commonly call for more substantial frames than other media. Mouldings must have positive character, but should be simple in profile, with decorative motifs according to good taste. A major requirement is that the frame be strong mechanically, and rigid enough to hold the canvas securely on its stretcher, to prevent warping or movement of the canvas that would eventually crack the paint.

WATERCOLORS Usually watercolor frames can be shallower, thinner, and more delicate than those used with oils. Wider mats are the rule. An important current change over past concepts is that many watercolors are strong enough to take heavy, well-textured frames instead of just solid bands. Watercolors invariably require glazing. French mats—mats that have decorative lines drawn around the "window"—also work well in some cases. To prevent buckling, and consequent distortion of the image, rag board plus a heavy cardboard should back most watercolors.

PASTELS Pastel drawings require frames similar to those for watercolors. The major exception is that some look best with little or no matting. Glass is required, but because

When framing an oil painting or reproduction, try to maintain or augment the dignity of the work. This portrait of Theodore Roosevelt presents an aura of strength with its deep blue frame and mat, relieved by elegant gold stripes.

pastels tend to smudge, the glass should be separated from the picture by a thin, usually concealed, insert. Pastel is the most delicate of all media and will continue to shed tiny powder grains, even after coated with a fixative. Both pastels and watercolors require a strong sheet at the back of the frame to seal out dirt.

GOUACHE Because of its physical kinship to watercolor, gouache requires much the same type of framing. Since the colors are opaque rather than transparent, however, most gouaches will require heavier, stronger looking frames than watercolors. Some techniques for painting with gouache produce an effect so similar to that of some oil paintings that frame treatment should be more like that of an oil than a watercolor. Glass is normally required.

PRINTS Lithographs, etchings, and woodcuts are commonly framed with narrow mouldings of natural wood or black or dark gray. Stark white matting should be avoided; a soft or off-white is better. Matting can be quite wide and deep, sometimes with a pertinent inscription related to the print. Glass is necessary for protection. Some prints, such as etchings and lithographs, have what is known as "plate mark." This is a rectangular depression, running around the print, caused by the pressure of the printing plate. It should not be hidden by the mat. When prints are signed, the signature should also be given plenty of space. Prints that have marking on the reverse side can have clear acetate or glass on the back to show the marking whenever desired. Many contemporary prints are being created in such strong patterns and colors that they demand important frames, such as might be used on oil paintings.

ORIGINAL DRAWINGS Their variety in style, size, and medium (pencil, silver point, pen, quill, brush) as well as the color of the drawing and paper, make generalization extremely difficult. Fortunately much greater attention is now given to the framing of drawings than in the past. This increased interest by museums and collectors has brought about a more serious and careful approach to the choice of the color, texture and size of the matting, as well as the width, style, and tonality of the frame.

PHOTOGRAPHIC PRINTS Matting is all-important with photographs, which can be treated effectively in several ways. Often, prints are mounted directly on the mounting or backing, with no moulding or glass. Others are best set off with some kind of moulding—usually stained or natural wood, gold, silver, or other metal.

Oils and acrylics rarely require mats. The wide dark wood moulding,
layered with golden insets, picks up the warm tones of this still life,
lending an air of weight and serenity to this painting.

Photographic portraits are also popular. They often hang in the living areas of a home, and they should, therefore, be framed with greater consideration.

MIRRORS There are two types of mirrors—those with clear glass that are actually functional; and those that are antique (or purposely antiqued), with glass in such condition that the overall effect is merely decorative. In either case, mirrors structurally and aesthetically lend themselves to heavy frames. A mirror is one art form in which the frame itself can be dominant. It is also far more dependent than any kind of picture on the surroundings for its particular style. It becomes in effect, more a piece of furniture than an object of art; and since its surface reflects part of its surroundings, there must be a closer tie between its frame and the architecture than in the case of a painting. Highly carved and ornate frames that are too overpowering for pictures often make excellent frames for mirrors. Keep in mind the relationship of the frame to the surroundings.

REPRODUCTIONS The first rule for reproductions—whether of oil paintings, watercolors, pastels, or prints—is treat them as originals when selecting the right frames. There are two slight differences, though, between a reproduction and an original. The first is an aesthetic one: a reproduction's color values may not have the strength or dimension of the original, and hence would be appropriate in a frame that is not too heavy. The second is a mechanical consideration: most reproductions have to be mounted (no matter what medium they represent) to prevent warping. In this case, they can be protected with varnish or sprayed lacquer so that no glass protection is needed. The selection of frame is highly important here (especially when the subject matter is such that the viewer knows it could not be an original), to avoid any impression of cheapness.

There are two schools of thought regarding the framing of reproductions: the one expressed above, that they should be treated as originals and another viewpoint that, since reproductions represent a brand new craft, they should be framed very simply.

Artist and critic Frederic Taubes takes a practical, in-between outlook, particularly in the matter of oils: "In contrast to frames for most oil paintings—which frames in general retain a rather conservative character—frames for color reproductions are most effective when they are somewhat novel in design."

THREE-DIMENSIONAL OBJECTS When it comes to other forms of art, such as sculpture, frames are generally considered either completely unnecessary or else

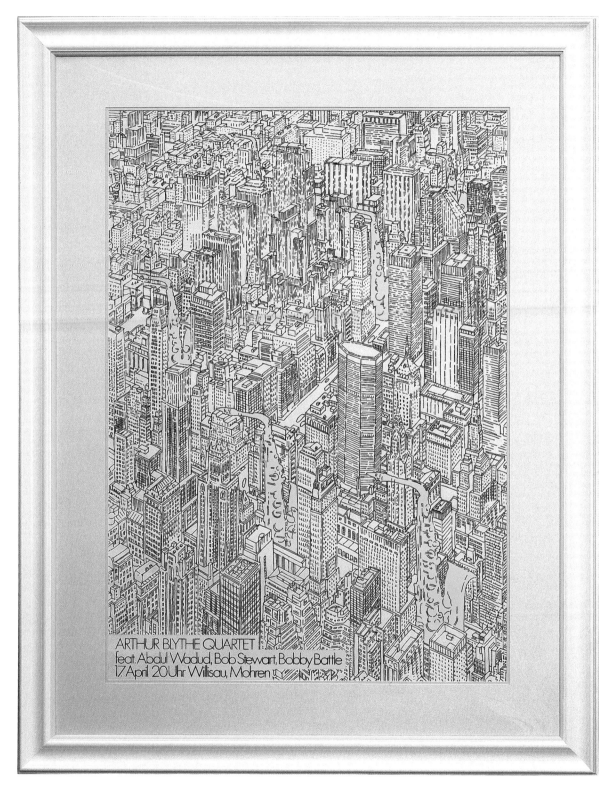

Elaborate frames should not overpower the strong graphic nature of poster art.

This cityscape maintains its integrity with a white frame and mat that merely hints

at the chrome yellow contained in the print.

59

actual drawbacks. Nevertheless, there are many instances in which framing can be employed effectively and tastefully. Salvador Dali's surrealist creations of precious stones are dramatically framed in mouldings with built-in lighting. Jewels, coins, medallions, flat sculptures, precious mementos, sports memorabilia—these are all examples of art and artistry that may be enhanced by the effective use of box frames.

Whatever consideration one may give to the beauty, art, and aesthetics of frame making, much of any decision concerning the "right" frame must be based on purely *material* conclusions. Such practical elements as mouldings and mats and inserts are as vital to the end result as are surface decorations and colors and other artistic embellishments. In this respect, a frame is like a piece of good furniture, which must have character and beauty, but which also must be physically suitable to its task without paying too much homage to the ravages of age, usage, and hard times.

The selection of the moulding by the frame maker plays an important part in the finish and decoration applied. There are, for instance, certain types of ornaments that traditionally go with certain types of mouldings—though there is no hard and fast rule.

A reputable frame-making shop will help you find the perfect setting for any artwork. Buying frames unseen, however, from a catalog or Internet source can be highly unsatisfactory—unless you know exactly what you want and what you will be getting ahead of time. There is nothing like trying on a suit of clothes before you buy—and the same applies to a good frame!

This unusual outwardly sloping gilt frame adds depth to the two-dimensional map print
without distracting from its Old World flavor.

Some Psychological Observations on Framing

Ludwig Richter relates in his reminiscences how once, when he was in Tivoli as a young man, he and three friends set out to paint part of the landscape, all four firmly resolved not to deviate from nature by a hair's-breadth; and al-though the subject was the same, and each quite creditably reproduced what his eyes had seen, the result was four totally different pictures, as different from each other as the personalities of the four painters. Whence the narrator drew the conclusion that there is no such thing as objective vision, and that form and color are always apprehended differently, according to temperament.

Here Heinrich Wolfflin in his *Principles of Art History* demonstrates briefly the differences in psychological outlook among artists. In art books, in histories, and in other works down through the ages, writers and authorities have constantly and zealously explored the psychological implications in paintings individually, in painting as a broad art, in sculpture, in music, and in just about every other field of artistic endeavor. But few, if any, seem to have so much as given a thought to such implications as they relate to framing and the picture frame.

◆   Why is a picture incomplete without a frame?

◆   Why does an unframed canvas on a wall disturb the viewer?

◆   Why does a frame in itself, with no picture contained inside, make you want to place something—anything—behind it to see what it looks like?

This chapter does not intend to furnish all the answers, but merely to make some observations that may be of interest in studying the nature of the picture frame and in applying principles right and wrong.

Why does a frame with no picture contained within it, immediately make you feel the need to place something—anything—inside it to see what it looks like?

The English author G. K. Chesterton approached one point of view when he wrote, "Art is limitation; the essence of every picture is the frame." It is like the cover and binding of a book. One says what one has to say, has the thoughts compressed within the limitations of leather or cloth for posterity to ponder, and then moves on to some other work.

Gertrude Stein was not so sure about any philosophy of limitation. "I like a picture, that is an oil painting to do anything it likes to do," she once said.

> The first thing that ever interested me in that way as the picture moving was the Leonardo in the Louvre, the Virgin, the Child and Saint Anne . . . in this picture there was an internal movement, not of the people or light or any of these things but inside in the oil painting. In other words, the picture did not live within the frame, in other words it did not belong within the frame. The Cézanne thing was different, it went further and further into the picture the life of the oil painting but it stayed put.

> I have thought a great deal about all this and I am still thinking about it. I have passionately hoped that some picture would remain out of its frame, I think it can even while it does not, even while it remains there. And this is the problem of all modern painting just as it has been the problem of all old painting. That is to say the first hope of a painter who really feels hopeful about painting is the hope that the panting will move, that it will live outside its frame.

In her own way, Stein has reflected a certain deep-rooted disturbance in the minds of many lovers of art: that there is a sense of security and well-being in seeing a picture strongly encompassed within its frame, or limitation, but that many pictures—like a tiger in a flimsy bamboo cage—do not seem to want to live within their prescribed confines.

One answer, though admittedly oversimplified, is that the right frame helps to make viewers secure in their enjoyment of a picture, whereas the wrong frame can unsettle them by giving the impression that the picture is either, a) being throttled and overpowered, or b) trying to bulge its way out of its surroundings.

Although the failure is not always easy to analyze, poor frames often arouse psychological misgivings when they are not in balance. Some painters are so concerned about this problem that they almost have an obsession about the relationship of the

To create a striking effect, try borrowing graphic elements from the artwork when composing the surround. In this example, the carved moulding echoes the shapes of Native American jewelry, while its rich bronze luster brings out the warmth of the sepia-toned photograph.

frame to one of their works. A number of years ago, the French painter Braitou-sala remarked about the frame, "The choice of its form, of its color and its material never leaves my thought while I am painting because it should be the prolongation of the work which is being born. One should construct the frame and the panting simultaneously so that they fuse so well in equilibrium that no one would think of separating them."

Portrait artist Albert Murray feels a great involvement with the frame, thinking of it as an extension of the painting. Often he will come into the frame-making shop to select a frame and then spend a great deal of time lovingly rubbing the moulding with his hands until it has exactly the patina he desires—something that cannot be described or specified in technical or trade terminology.

Moise Kisling regarded frames as a kind of challenge. He liked nothing better than to select a superbly carved frame, set it up on his easel with a bare canvas inside and then reverse the accepted procedure by letting the frame dictate the composition and coloring of the painting he would execute.

One prominent art collector, Henry Pearlman, has been known to hang large expanses of wall with nothing but empty frames. When asked why he does this, he replies, "I think they're beautiful. They were done by hand, by real artisans who had *time*—not rushed like you and me." Pearlman's approach is both imaginative and inventive—he has one large frame that contains not one, but seven Cézanne drawings—but it evidences the appeal that frames hold for many people.

There is definitely an emotional quality about frames that give them personality and help to attract or repel the viewer. As an associate once put it in a light moment, "Frames can be sad or funny; voluptuous like a woman or severe like a Puritan preacher; warm and flexible as fine cloth, or cold and brittle as an icicle."

In studying frames, you can often feel some of the emotion coming through, thus adding to, or detracting from, the emotion of the picture within. A frame that is light, buoyant, and lively quite naturally would fit a picture that has the same qualities, but would clash harshly with a picture that happened to be serious, somber, intellectual. Frequently a frame that is highly appropriate for a picture will have absolutely no appeal for a viewer, not because the frame is wrong, but because the viewer is not sympathetic with the mood and feeling expressed. The chances are, in a case like this, that he will not be greatly taken by the picture either.

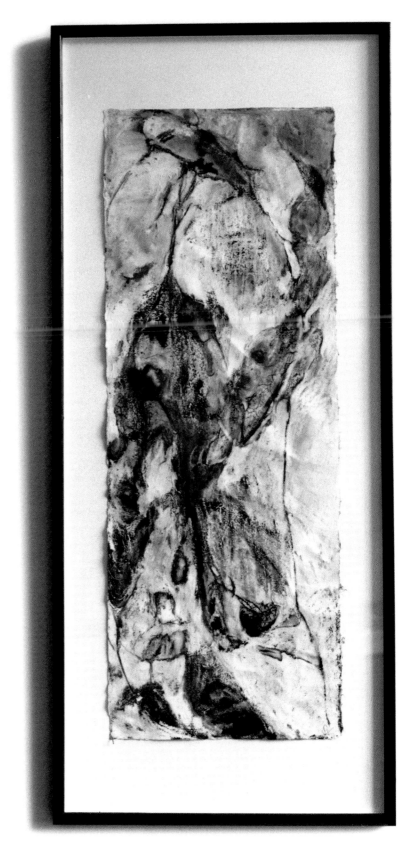

In this oil pastel by Nathalie Guarracino, we see restless movement being contained by a stark black frame. Most abstract art benefits from simple, uncomplicated frames that let the artwork do the talking.

There is one further function of the frame that might be referred to loosely as being "psychological" as well as practical, and that is its employment for protective purposes. Normally, glass is not used on a frame for an oil or acrylic painting. In the case of an antique oil or one that, for any reason, has started to deteriorate, however, a special frame is required that does have glass on the front and a sealer on the back. "A great deal can be done to protect a picture by housing it in a suitable frame," explains Stout. "Observations over a period of about thirty years have given good reason to believe that paintings set into a frame which is, in effect, an airtight box have held their condition far better than similar works exposed to the air. Such a frame need not be heavy or cumbersome. It needs to have the glass sealed, to have the face of the picture some distance behind that, and to have an airtight backing. This framing keeps out dirt, it protects the picture from minor accidents, it keeps out water, and it reduces extreme and rapid changes of temperature and relative humidity."

This represents the ultimate in protection for a picture. Beyond that, it also furnishes a certain subtle and not easily defined sense of security that is appreciated by viewers as well as by the picture's owner.

Again, we see this symbolic representation of the frame as an element that protects art, because it is elusive, not easily defined and usually related to the emotions, flourishes best when it is securely confined, protected, and psychologically satisfying.

Displaying photographs of friends and family fulfills a psychological need to show off the ones we love. Here the right frame honors the subject of a small black-and-white photograph. While adhering to the tradition of using white mats and black frames for photos, this one also adds impact by the choice of a wide mat surrounded by an inward slanting wood-grain moulding.

Chronology in Its Proper Perspective

"We are going to take a Velázquez and frame it in an adaptation of a Régence moulding."

"I want you to see that drawing by Matisse, done in the 1920s. It is hung in a wide, simple nineteenth-century American frame."

Fifty years or so ago, both of these remarks would have brought gasps of dismay from a large coterie of experienced art critics. You just did not consider anything but a Spanish Renaissance frame for a Velázquez! And whoever heard of putting a twentieth-century French work in an American frame designed for the preceding century?

Yet both of the works mentioned were at home in frames from different periods and different countries.

History runs in cycles, and every so often the so-called "purists" are in the vanguard, selling the notion that any kind of a mixture is bastardization or mongrelization and not suitable for the world of art. Fortunately, today, the trend is toward considering each situation individually, although many museums and collectors still do strive for strict historical accuracy when exhibiting paintings or any other art form.

Much worse than this striving for purism is the practice that has come into vogue again and again in the history of painting: discarding all of the old frames in a collection of Old Masters and replacing them with whatever happened to be currently in style. We have seen what resulted when Napoleon went overboard for Empire gold, and this unhappy act has many parallels in history—both before and after the Emperor's time.

Mixing time periods can add spice when composing your artwork. This example shows how opposites attract--even though the images are of a classical column layered over a page of Latin script, the frame treatment is very contemporary.

Quite a few instances can be pointed out when the right frame is definitely not one from the artwork's own particular period. One of the best examples would be the case of a masterful painting or reproduction from the mid-Victorian period. It would be all but ruined today, as it probably was when it was painted, by being smothered in one of the plush, sentimental, and multi-mouldinged monstrosities of the period.

Between the extremes of historical fussery and brash regimentation there lies a zone of reason that should guide anyone in the selection of framing: Frames for old pictures should be selected with a thoughtful respect for the period in which they were painted, with a consequent adherence to the spirit of good framing as practiced during that period. But allowances should also be made for current tastes, and to a certain degree, technologies. If a particular motif popular in one era has since that time come to have a distorted, even objectionable, meaning, it obviously should not be used in a current design. The swastika is perhaps the most dramatic example—a perfectly honest, popularized design in ancient Greece, Persia, and even back to the Bronze Age—that was turned into such a symbol of hate by the Nazis that its use in a frame moulding would undoubtedly give the picture a meaning never intended.

Technology influences taste to the degree that an antique frame designed for use in a candlelit hall of 200 years ago would produce a somewhat different effect when hung in a your living room today. Does that old frame do the same thing for an antique painting as it once did? Or is it perhaps better to effect a modification, retaining the spirit and feeling, but possibly enfolding the composition more protectively and shielding it from some of the harshness that has crept into our modern decor?

In the matter of chronology, too little attention has been given to related factors: *geography* and *climate*. When you walk into a room, you enter from an outside environment. You may not think about it, but that environment definitely influences your interest in, and affinity for, various items, furnishings, furniture, art, and other elements within an interior. Let us say that you have entered a living room after several hours spent outside, in desert country, in 100-degree heat. Your eye, your body, your thoughts will be attracted more by an airy, lightweight chair textured in cool green than by a dark, heavy, poreless armchair that looks as though it might stifle you in its grasp.

A spare, minimalist frame highlights the timeless appeal of this simple graphic,

a Zen Buddhist symbol.

Conversely, if you walk into an inn after a cold drive through heavy snow, you are more likely to make your way to a dark, weighty table that is candlelit and has substantial chairs than to a wrought-iron ensemble near the sun porch that is surrounded by cool green plants.

Pictures and frames should be selected with at least some reflection on geographical and climatic environment. Subject matter, composition, style, and other factors will be strengthened to a certain degree by the manner in which they are complemented by the surroundings—even the surroundings beyond the confines of the room in which they hang.

*This paper collage creates the effect of a tribal mask and is appropriately framed
with wood panels that evoke the feeling of bamboo.*

The Fine Art of Hanging Pictures

Not long ago, a couple visited a prominent frame maker to select exactly the right frames for five oil paintings and two watercolors. It took them something like two weeks and a dozen visits to the studio before they were convinced that they had selected the proper frames.

The happy ending to this little story should have been that the couple proudly hung them in their duplex apartment where they were right at home and admired by one and all.

Not so.

As it turned out, the pictures had been purchased as part of a decorating project: to fill a large expanse of white wall in the living room, an area that had proven to be quite an artistic challenge. The wife had decided that "six or seven pictures" would do the trick, and the husband had further opined that the pictures would have to be genuinely fine art, expensive, and superbly framed in the best of taste.

By the time the pictures had been duly arranged and hung they formed such a conglomeration of art that, instead of attracting admiring attention, they simply served as a kind of pleasant and colorful pattern, to which few guests ever paid any attention. Furthermore, two of the pictures were so high on the wall that they were properly viewable only when standing on a chair; one required a weed-picker's stoop to look at from a feasible angle; and none had proper lighting.

The moral of this little tale is that you can have the finest works of art in the most suitable frames, but then sabotage their effectiveness by hanging them, or regrouping them, in a ridiculous manner.

RIGHT *When you are decorating an intimate conversation area, it helps to keep your artwork low and accessible, as shown here in this cozy study.*

There are two reasons for hanging pictures: The first is to exhibit fine art properly, under circumstances where it can be studied and admired to the fullest extent; the second (and perfectly valid) reason is simply to provide a form of decoration. In the latter case, however, it is wasteful—indeed, an example of very poor taste—to sacrifice *valuable* works of art and carefully designed frames just to achieve a decorative effect that ranks no higher than that of the wallpaper or the pattern on the draperies.

As artist Van Day Truex once wrote, "Comparatively unimportant paintings and drawings can achieve gaiety and freshness when framed effectively with large mats, imaginatively colored and textured, or with cheerful mouldings upholstered in anything from felt to chintz. But don't get your serious pictures mixed up with this philosophy. . . ."

So group, group to your heart's content when you are hanging mere illustrations, but be careful when it comes to real art!

One basic dictate for hanging paintings precludes the possibility that you can group them properly, except in the most unusual circumstances: A good picture should be hung low. If you do not believe this, take a little time to observe where many people hang a picture—over the mantel. If the picture is landscape, you will probably find that you cannot even look at it at all well without being clear across the room. Or, if you want to examine detail, you have to get up close and crane your neck.

Small pictures should be hung approximately at eye level, rather than lower, because their detail can be clearly seen without physical strain. No picture should be hung in a position where close inspection is impossible, which means that, whereas you might hang a large picture with large detail over a couch, this position would not be wise for a picture with minute detail, where the viewer would have to bend over awkwardly to try to inspect it at close range.

Remember, too, that pictures hung in a hall, where people are normally *standing*, require different positioning from those hung in a dining or living room where people spend most of the time *seated*.

Not many years ago, it was considered acceptable to hang pictures, particularly large, heavy paintings, from wire or cord that extended upward to the "picture molding" at the ceiling. In fact, just about every house built before World War II traditionally had picture moldings in the main rooms. This method, while perhaps easier on the wall, distracts from the picture. In the case of large paintings, it emphasizes the physi-

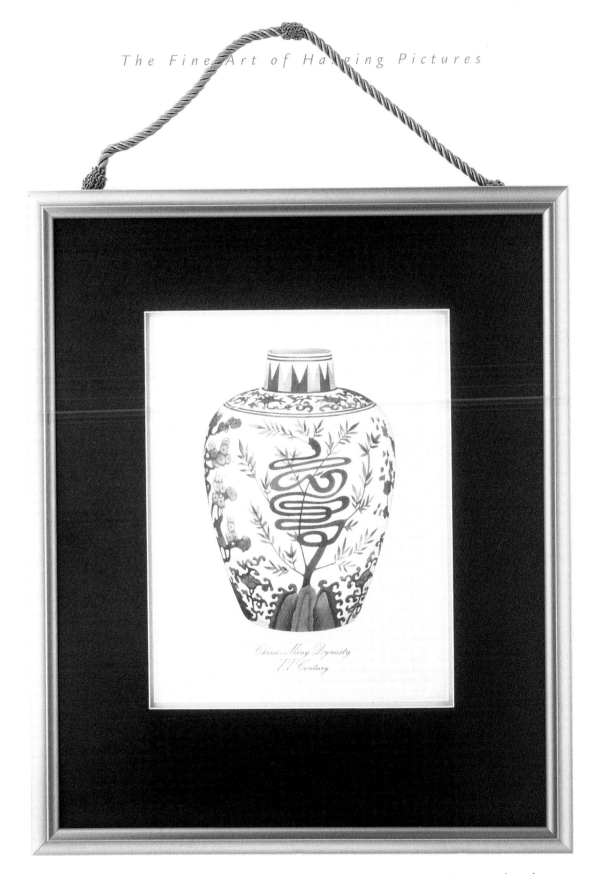

Rather than distracting from the impact of this porcelain vase print, the exposed cord picks up the gold tones from the gilt moulding.

cal weight of the whole, and often kills the effect of a composition that is light and airy. In the case of small paintings, such support looks incongruous.

The only way to affix a painting to the wall is in the most unobtrusive manner possible, by using picture nails and hooks—preferably two for each picture, spaced about three-fourths of the width of the entire frame apart, to prevent slipping into a crooked position. The wire and hooks should never be visible from any position a viewer might take.

When selecting the positions that various pictures will have on various walls, there are two other important considerations to bear in mind:

Have you allowed a realistic viewing vista? That is, can people see the picture at the proper distance, and with enough leeway so that someone really interested can look at the picture from both the right and the left, as well as in the middle? A good picture will bear observation from a dozen different positions, and some will reward the viewer by providing a slightly different effect from each viewpoint.

Have you taken the composition into consideration when selecting the location? Some compositions are more at home at the right end of a wall; some at the left; some in the middle. Probably the simplest example to demonstrate this principle is that of a portrait that is in profile. If the head is pointing toward the *left*, the frame should be hung somewhere to the right of center of the wall, since the composition tends to give movement in the direction that the subject's eyes are looking. Such a picture might effectively be hung far toward the right end of the wall; but it would be disturbing at the left end, where it would seemingly be staring into the corner.

The final element for consideration is space.

A picture has to form a focal point, without distracting objects or decorations above, below, on either side, or in front of it. Some paintings require more space than others, and the amount is by no means determined by the size of the frame. A quiet still life can happily occupy a smaller space than a colorful, lively carnival scene or an angry seascape. Subdued colors do not absorb as much of the surrounding wall as do bright and vibrant ones, as in the case of a brilliant abstract.

RIGHT   *When creating a wall grouping, it is more effective to frame each piece according to its own requirements, than to frame them all alike. This avoids giving the grouping a static uniformity.*

Whatever this book says, or fails to say, it is intended only as a guide, in a field that has been too little studied by the art world, and in which there are astonishingly few reference works of any length or in any language. When it comes right down to analyzing the art of framing, and to distinguishing the rights from the wrongs, the best general advice that can be given is absurdly simple in essence:

Try it out and see.

Check out one frame against another; style against style, period against period. Have the patience to live with a painting or other picture for a while before taking what is really an important step with any real work of art—selecting the proper frame that will bring out its best qualities, whether you are framing an original Picasso or your daughter's fingerpainting. And when it comes to selecting the frame, choose it with all the care and consideration that you used when selecting the picture in the first place.

RIGHT   *A subtle graphic is hung so that standing viewers can study it. The sleek modern frame with a wide mat adds a dramatic effect, while echoing the sleek cool tones of the living room.*

Resources

For further information on the frames featured on pages 4, 15, 19, 21, 23, 23, 25, 27, 29, 31, 33, 35, 37, 39, 41, 43, 45, 47, 51, 53, 55, 57, 59, 61, 65, 69, 71, 75, and 81, please contact:

Art & Framing Council
Kim Aherne, Executive Director
501 Maggiore Court
Brentwood, CA 94513
925.516.0313
www.artandframingcouncil.org

Aaron Brothers Art & Framing
1270 S. Goodrich Boulevard
Commerce, CA 90022
888.532.9372
www.aaronbrothers.com

Aesthetic Frame & Art Service
8221 Melrose Avenue
Los Angeles, CA 90046
323.653.9033

Albany Frameworks
2520 Dawson Road
Albany, GA 31707
912.889.1423
www.albanyframeworks.com

Art & Framing Council
20715 Driftwood Court
Mundelein, IL 60060
847.566.1722
www.artandframingcouncil.org

Art & Picture Framing Inc.
5511 Bergenline Avenue
West New York, NJ 07093
201.865.0430

ARTFRAME
Brookview Village Center
1218 Hill Road N.
Pickerington, OH 43147
614.868.5554
www.artframeit.com

The Artshoppe
23 S. Willson
Bozeman, MT 59715
406.586.8696
www.frameitup.com

Belle Frames Ltd
1647 1st Avenue
New York, NY 10028
212.737.4778

Bennett Smith Framing & Restoration
170 Palisade Avenue
Cliffside Park, NJ 07010
201.840.8444

Buffalo Picture Frame
3229 Main Street
Buffalo, NY 14202
716.838.3800
www.bufflopictureframe.com

Cape Cod Picture Framing
780 Main Street
Dennis, MA 02638
508.385.5482
www.ccpf.com

Cardinal Frame & Art
1904 Ranch Road 12, Ste 101
San Marcos, TX 78666
512.392.7699
www.sanmarcos.net/cardinalframe

Cathy's Picture Framing
8240 Mayfield Road
Chesterland, OH 44026
440.729.8191
www.cathyspictureframingandgallery.com

Charrette Corporation
331 Olympia Avenue
Woburn, MA 01888
800.367.3729
www.charrette.com

Dakota Framing Specialties
P.O. Box 485
Watertown, SD 57201
605.886.2555
www.dakotaframingspecialties.com

Deck the Walls
100 Glenborough Drive
Houston, TX 77067
888.286.3988
www.deckthewalls.com

Evergreen Framing Co & Gallery
2019 E. 3300 Street
Salt Lake City, UT 84109
801.467.8770
www.omana.com

F & D Frame Co
693 Anderson Avenue
Cliffside Park, NJ 07010
201.945.0882

Fame Frame Co
938 4th Avenue S.
Nashville, TN 37210
615.254.4278

Fast Frame
1200 Lawrence Drive, Ste 300
Newbury Park, CA 91320
805.498.4463
www.fastframe.com

4 Corners Picture Framing
270 Littleton Road
Olde Boston Square #19
Westford, MA 01886
978.692.8535
www.westford.com/4corners

frame crafter
P. O. Box 398922
Miami Beach FL 33239
305.975.6366
www.framecrafter.com

Framerica
2 Todd Court
Yaphank, NY 11980
800.372.6422
www.framerica.com

The Framer's Workshop
2439 Channing Way
Berkeley, CA 94704
510.849.4444
www.framersworkshop.com

Frametastic
Box 2263
124 King Street West
Prescott, ON Canada K0E 1T0
613.925.1273
www.frametastic.com

Framing Fox Art
148 Main Street
Lebanon, NJ 08833
800.237.6077
www.framingfox.com

Frantic Framers
1592 Hancock Street
Quincy, MA 02169
617.479.4352
www.aad1.com/franticframers

The Great Frame Up
100 Glenborough Drive
Houston, TX 77067
800.55.FRAME
www.thegreatframeup.com

Henry H. Taws
1527 Walnut Street
Philadelphia, PA 19102
215.563.6324

Horizon Fine Arts
Centennial Plaza
5502 Lawrence Avenue E.
Toronto, ON Canada
416.284.2900
www.horizonfinearts.com

Larson-Juhl
www.larsonjuhl.com

LivingStone Picture Framing
1060 Highway 14 East
Janesville, WI 53545
608.754.2767
www.livingstonepictureframing.com

Martin & MacArthur
Picture Frame Mouldings
1815 Kahai Street
Honolulu, HI 96819
800.845.0099
www.martinandmacarthur.com

Metropolitan Picture Framing
6959 Washington Ave. South
Minneapolis, MN 55439
800.626.3139
www.metroframe.com

Michaels.com
850 N. Lake Drive
Coppell, TX
800.MICHAELS
www.michaels.com

Neilson Bainbridge
40 Eisenhower Drive
Paramus, NJ 07652
800.656.6853
www.neison-bainbridge.com

Pacific Picture Framing
318 N. Olympic
Arlington, WA 98223
360.435.2982
www.pacificpictureframing.com

Pearson Moulding & Supply
314 E. 11th Street
Erie, PA 16503
800.458.7607
www.pearsonmoulding.com

Picture Perfect of Nora Corners
1484 E. 86th Street
Indianapolis, IN 46240
877.755.2600
www.customframer.com

Port Townsend Frame Works
823 Water Street
Port Townsend, WA 98368
360.385.3809
www.viewit.com/FrameWorks

Professional Picture Framers Association
4305 Sarellen Road
Richmond, VA 23231
800.556.6228
www.ppfa.com

R. C. Danon Gallery
1124 Central Avenue
Wilmette, IL 60091
847.256.5612
www.danonartframes.com

Rocky Mountain Art & Framing
821 Acoma Street #C
Denver, CO 80204
303.446.9195
www.rockymountainart.com

Sam Flax
425 Park Avenue
New York, NY 10022
800.SAMFLAX
www.samflax.com

Southern Moulding & Supply Co.
7040 Battle Drive
Kennesaw, GA 30152
770.422.3949
www.southernmoulding.com

Steinway Gallery
1289 N. Fordham Boulevard
Chapel Hill, NC 27514
919.942.8780

Studio Moulding
www.studiomouldinginc.com

Universal Framing Products
12432 Foothill Boulevard
Sylmar, CA 91342
800.668.3627
www.universalframing.com

Weems Prinz Framing
2445 Chelwood Park Boulevard
Albuquerque, NM 87112
505.298.9082
www.wrldcon.com/weems

The Williamson Co.
800.851.2467
www.williamsonco.com

You've Been Framed
3275 W. Ali Baba Lane
Las Vegas, NV 89118
702.597.9456